Introduction

I am sitting here at the table, gazing out of the window, as I write the sky is silvery grey, snow has fallen on the ground, light dustings of it on brown tiled roof tops, resembling icing sugar on gingerbread houses. Icicles balance upon the hedgerows they twinkle in the sun like a crystal necklace as the sun shines through the chinks in the clouds.

I am deep in thought I hear the familiar tick tock from the London quartz company clock. It is a deep resonant sound tick tock, tick tock, tick tock. It is comforting yet disconcerting; it is a reminder of fading youth a clock is a symbol of mortality. This clock is the same one that had pride of place upon our mum's mantelpiece.

We inherit time, the very essence of life is time every moment every second, breathing is time, time is the most precious gift of all. Once time is gone the moment has disappeared. We are left with only memories those memories of joy or sadness.

We hope to keep our memories the ones that give meaning to our lives. The tragedy of Alzheimer's erased our parent's memories. We hope to hold onto the things we remember, yet some of us are not that lucky.

My brother and I became that woman or that man, our mum, my dad and my nan all suffered the same cruel fate of developing dementia, for years my dad, took on the responsibility of caring for my nan, I saw how it had broken his spirit throughout the years as he witnessed his mums decline. As for our mum she had forgotten that she had a son or daughter at all.

We observed with horror, as we watched our parents being destroyed by dementia robbing them of their vitality the mischievous sparkle in their eyes, it was devastating to see them being turned into an empty shell a husk a shuffling zombie, until they lost the use of their legs.

To see our once so proud and dignified parents having to be spoon fed and toileted like a baby was harrowing. It felt like a knife slicing through our hearts over and over then dragged out slowly extending the pain, it felt like a kind of death to my brother, and I. Something died in us.

We lost part of ourselves, yet through it all we had to find the strength to carry on through the anguish. So, this is what compelled me to write this book, I wish to help others find their strength too. When my dad died, I heard his voice it said do something amazing with your writing.

The book is a special collection of my poems and poems my dad wrote. He often put these poems in birthday and Christmas cards to me, the title of this book is Wings of a Butterfly, the Butterfly is a symbol of the joy, hope, love and beauty of the human spirit, its wings are delicate much like memories we treasure of those we hold close to our hearts.

There is another reason for the title of this book, my dad gave gifts to me of butterfly jewellery and butterfly's on birthday cards, when I look back at all of these collections of cards, I now realise he was trying to tell me something, I think he saw me as his little caterpillar, turning into a chrysalis and then emerging as an adult butterfly, to spread her wings and fly off into the world.

Juliette Trevett

Copyright © 2024 Juliette Trevett. All rights reserved.
Published by Juliette Trevett Publishing
ISBN 978-1-7385660-0-6

Poems

4	The Rose
5	Being of Light
6	Something Beautiful
7	Star Seed
8	The Tree
9	Dance
10	Guardian Angel
11	Love Dies
12	The Eagle
13	The Wolf
14	Dawn
15	Breeze
16	I am the Stillness
17	The Naturist
18	Birds
19	Seeds
20	The Kitten
21	The Butterfly
22	Sunflowers and Rainbows
23	How would they feel
24	A picnic with Daddy
28	The Forest
29	Forget-Me-Not
30	A Rainbow has appeared the Forget-Me-Not's have Grown
32	The Pheonix

Dad's Poems

35	A Daughter
36	By the Fireside
37	The Fly
38	The Phantom Coach
39	The Cat
40	The Spell
41	Snow
42	The Cathedral
43	The Forest of Never
45	Kittie's Plight

The Rose

She is caressed by the touch of the evening sun above.
Her deep crimson petals trembling.
In the presence of his love.

The Rose, her time does not last.
With every day she is growing older.
Her life is far too short.
Such beauty cannot be outclassed.

Autumn leaves they fall.
The sky darkens.
Mourning natures call.
Death for all.

Now the seasons have gone away.
To become another year's summer day.
Her exquisite gown of red now faded.
The rose hangs her head.
Jaded.

Her Petals.
Falling.
Falling.
Disintegrating.
In her shame.
She was once Queen of flowers.
The Rose was her name.

<u>Being of Light</u>

We are beings of shimmering light.
Twinkling Auras.
Ever changing.
Evolving.
Bright.
Day.
Night.

Something Beautiful

Something beautiful.
Something lost.
Something beautiful inside of our soul.
Something magical, tender.
Ethereal.
A glimpse of fairyland mystery & wonder.

Like a delicate seed, escaping from a dandelion clock.
It floats away.
Far away in the distance carried by the direction of the wind.

Like a sweet scent of wallflowers after the rain.
Like a dream never to return.
Or remember upon waking.

Something beautiful.
Like the particles of shimmering dust Reflecting through a sunbeam.
Like the rainbow that's fading on the horizon.
Something beautiful disappeared.
Childhoods end.

Star Seed

I am a Starseed.
Born from love.
Blessed from moon beams above.

The Beauty of the Earth.
Captures my heart.
My soul held in the hand of God's grace.
Natures colours.
The purest art.

I am sunlight.
A glowing ray.
The mystery of night.
Dawning of the day.

<u>The Tree</u>

Majestic in his glory.
He is adorned with a crown of green & gold.
Shimmering in the light of the Autumn Sunset.

His magnificence takes my breath away.
I am humbled by his opulence.
As I rest my cheek against his solid comforting trunk.

His magical energy awakens my soul.
I hear his whispers hushed.
Telling stories from legends past.

Dance

Come, Come, Dance.
Dance to the rhythm of the wild sea.
The power of creation that be.

Come, Come, Dance.
To the kiss of the silvery moon.
Peaking from behind the dusky clouds in June.

Come, Come, Dance.
To the feeling within your soul.
Love Awakening your heart.
Like an arrow.
Like a dart.

Come, Come, Dance.
To the rhythm of Earths beating drum.
The flowers, raindrops the silent hum.

Come, Come, Dance.
To the rhythm of the storm.
Changing colours in the sky.
As they transform.

Come, Come, Dance.
To the rhythm of the birds in flight.
Dance.
Dance.
Dance.
To the wonder of the Universe.
A beautiful sight.

Guardian Angel

I have an Angel by my side.
Her loving arms encircle me.
She loves me unconditionally.

Her soft voice is heard in my solitude.
There is no need to fear.
She has blessed me.

Her kiss is sweet upon my head.
My Angel is here.

Love Dies

An Anguished scream of pain.
Loves arms reached out to her lover, hope.
She pleaded with him to save her.
He laughed in her soft beautiful innocent face.

Tears trickled down her flushed cheeks.
Her heart ceased to beat.
Hope stood before her his dark green eyes glittering with evil.
As he watched love die.

Then passion the hero of the night.
Rode upon his steed.
His kind compassionate eyes sparkling in the moon light.

He gazed down seeing love lying dead.
He bent to kiss loves sweet red lips.
He gave her life again.
She smiled shyly.
She ran away to find her home.
The heart.

The Eagle

Wind, Rain Thunder.
Eagle hovering through the turbulence of the storm.
Still she rises.
From mountain peaks under.

Souring through cumulous clouds.
Sunrise Sky.
Magnificent wings flying high.

She dips and dives.
Swooping into cool rivers below.
To catch her prey.
It cannot be from yesterday.

Her eyes open wide.
Solitude her salvation.
Poised on a rock edge.
Gazing down at the nation

She hides away in a cave.
Dank.
Dark.
Her skin bleeding.
In her nest she will stay.
To be reborn.

Feathers anew.
Her beauty & grace.
She flies once again.
To take her regal place.

The Wolf

Moon is mistress of the night.
The wolf is prowling.
His eyes flickering bright.
He stays away from mankind.
Safety there he could not find.

A chill in the air.
The stars reflection in his steely stare.

The Heartbeat of the earth.
The call of the wild.
Flows through his silvery veins.
Watching.
Waiting.
From behind forest trees.
In the torrential rains.

In the distance standing upon the jagged rock.
The howl of the beast is heard throughout Languadoc.

Dawn

A spiders Web.
Woven with care.
Hanging.
Suspended.
In the Air.

Wide eyed deer with her doe.
Waking in the woodland.
Brown eyes glow.

Speckled thrush.
Flutters her wing.
Dawn has arrived.
Hear her sing.

Morning is coming.
From the passing of the Moon.
From behind the clouds.
The sun will rise soon.

Breeze

Gentle is the breeze.
He blows softly over me.
With his cool breath.
Embracing me.
Every inch of my body.

He plays with my long blonde hair.
Whispering in my ears.
Tickling my ear lobes.

Together we run.
Throughout the lush green meadows.
Adorned with the wildflowers.
My Soul belongs to him.

My dress is captured.
Within his cold hand.
Together we laugh.
Without inhibitions.
Without restraint.
I cannot but love his mischievous abandon.

<u>I am the Stillness</u>

I am the stillness,
The lull between the break of thunder,

I am the quietness,

The calmness,
Gentle ripples upon a stream,
Flowing in many directions,

The Naturist

I am free.
An Eve walking through her garden of wildflowers.

I am joyful.
Without Shame.

For what can I be ashamed of.
I am as God created me.

Our mother earth is also exposed.
Naked.
Yet Glorious!

The Sun he kissed me.
My body tingled.
I felt his glow.
His Love.

A smile touched the corner of my lips.
I cannot help but love him back.

Birds

I dwell inside my mind.
I am sitting beneath the chestnut tree.

I Look up and see a Little Robin.
I sigh oh to have wings.

So I could fly.
Birds messengers from heaven.
Souls set free.

One day a bird.
Will take place of me.

Seeds

The seeds of love.
Lie Dormant within.
Deeply Buried inside of the Heart.

The tender kiss.
A loving touch.
Like the Vibration of the sun.

That ignites the flowers to bloom.
Into the abundant garden.
Bursting forth in a kaleidoscope of colours.

The Kitten

Friend come play with me.
Tickle my belly
It feels nice you see.
I bite your fingers.
Jump upon your back.
Independent am I.
I follow no pack.

You human of mine.
Caress my soft head.
As I stretch my spine.
I am loyal to you for ever more
I pat you gently with my paw.

I curl peacefully upon your lap.
Purring loudly as I take my nap.
You give me treats when I am good.
Stray from you I never would.

I lie in the sunbeams.
Upon your bed
Contented.
Happy.
And fed.

The Butterfly

They turned their face away from her.
The caterpillar, ugly, Unseen.
Upon a leaf in a field green.
Flower petals, tattered, torn.
Spring passed.
She shed her skin.
A queen from her chrysalis is born.

How precious, the butterfly.
Her heart beats her last day.
This miracle of beauty will die.
She lights up my smile.
Between the tears I cry.
As she flies on her way.

Her wings gossamer in sunlight.
Is she of this world.
Or a fairy in flight.
She flits from flower to flower.
More exhausted by the hour.
Hovering in the air.
Like a fading dream.
Tomorrow, she won't be there.

Sunflowers and Rainbows

I sit here in my garden.
Surrounded by the glory of the day.
The sunflower stands tall.
The rain has brought a rainbow my way.

Oh, rainbow what a gift you are to me.
Like a satin ribbon stretched across the sky.
I wish I was a bird.
So, I could fly.

The Pretty colours are bright.
The Sparrow I see taking flight.
A gentle breeze lifts my hair.
The sun peeps from behind the clouds.
Like a shy child.
Hiding from the Crowds.

How would they feel

The Earth is crying.
Her Green once luscious forests dying.
Rain.
Tears
Chemical cocktail, fears.
Descending down on to the flowers.
Humankind.
Loosing hours.

How would they feel.
No more War.
To turn away from what they saw.
No Nuclear bomb.
Destruction.
Of Sea, Land.
Will they never understand.

Poachers come, carrying their guns.
Massacring creatures of beauty.
In the name of greed.
Money.
Duty.

Our Earth.
A sacred masterpiece of wonder.
Do they ever stop to ponder.
And if they did how would they feel?
Our planets pain is all too real.

A picnic with Daddy

A meadow upon the edge of Lichfield town.
A green goddess wears her crown.
Summer of nineteen seventy-six, ages past.
Childhood was not to last.
Daddy's hand warm and strong.
To Pipegreen we walked along.

A piggyback upon my daddy's shoulder.
Could he take the pace.
He was getting older.
There in the distance a little cottage and a brook.
Like Nutwood common from the Rupert Bear book.

Footsteps through the wildflowers.
Sacred hours.
Pineapple weed.
Tiny seed
Daisies sweet.
Daddy put me back on my little feet.
Humming of bumble bee
A cabbage white butterfly we did see.

There it was the perfect place.
Excitement upon my little face.
Daddy now out of breath.
Many years later his death.

He pulls out the tempting pack.
From the carrier Bag of his rucksack.
Home baked bread.

Crusty and delicious.
Spread with creamy farmhouse butter.
With happiness my little heart did flutter.
Cheddar cheese.
More daddy please.

Pickled onions.
Crunchy crisps.
Melting in my mouth.
Birdsong from the south.

Beneath the bridge.
A little spring running clear.
A dragonfly to appear.
We removed our shoes.
Bare feet in the summer heat.

We drank Cherryade.
Time causes everything to fade.
In the distance.
Lemonsley wood farm.
The scent of flowers mingled with poo.
Oh what could I do.
I wrinkled my little nose.
Trying to recompose hope it goes.

A bleating sheep.
A curious cow mooing.
What on earth were those humans doing.

Daddy picked a buttercup.
Held it beneath my little chin.

"Do you like butter"
I grin.
He told me of the flowers from every hue.
Rare beauties of Pipegreen.
A wondrous sight to be seen.

Daddy and I paddled in the brook.
His jeans rolled up to his hairy Knees.
A soft warm breeze whispering through the trees.

Warm water lapping at my toes.
Footprint patterns in the sand.
Holding on to daddy's loving hand.

From the fishing net.
Lively wiggling tadpoles in the water.
Precious time with his little daughter.
We let them go upon their way.
They will be a frog when we return another day.

Little fish swimming beneath the stones.
He told me about the cuttlefish from up the stream.
The suns twinkling light diamonds on the water to beam.

A cow found my flip flop a tasty treat.
Daddy shouted No! No!
Bolting up the bank.
Wet feet!
Flip flop rescued.
A little chewed.

What a spectacle to see.

Families laughing with glee.
Daddy waved the flip flop in the air.
As more children gathered to stare.

Time to leave the play and walk on.
Climb over the stye.
Daddy feeds an apple to the horse in the field nearby.

The sun now fading.
Going down.
Walking Home.
Evening appears.
Daddy took away all my fears.
The joy ended all too soon.
We glimpsed the golden Moon.

The Forest

I sit in quiet contemplation.
I hear the orchestra of nature's sweet music.
Wood pigeon coos.
Tawny owl hooting.
A bird song chorus.

Trees sway side to side in a soft whispering breeze.
Leaves sparkle, shimmering like sequins in the beam of the midday sun.
The ripple upon the lake, building to a crescendo as it sends vibrations through the forest.
Pretty iridescent winged damsel flies hover.

Yellow and white daffodils perk up their trumpet heads in celebration of the spring.
Surrounding a carpet of bluebell pixie hats.
A gaggle of geese.
A quacking duck.
A mother goose sitting upon her eggs arranging feathers and pinecones for their bed.
Tucking them in with her beak.
Mothers safe cocoon.

Squirrels hop into the undergrowth.
And up the trees.
A rabbit scurries, a bumblebee buzzes.
A butterfly flits, wings flutter.
A doe with her wide-eyed fawn.
Fragrant wildflowers Daisies and dandelions, abundant.

Forget-Me-Not

Forever in my dreams,
Only you were the sunshine,
Reminders everywhere,
Grief,
Everything is precious,
Trying to find the strength,

Memories,
Eternity,

Nostalgia,
One day we will meet again,
Tears,

A Rainbow has appeared the Forget-Me-Not's have grown

The final goodbye was yesterday.
To Heaven you were sent.
The angels welcomed you into their loving arms.
Of unconditional love.
A rainbow has appeared.
The Forget-me-nots have grown.

The sorrow has turned to longing.
I will never hold you again on earth.
Or feel your strength when I was drowning in a sea of chaos.
You reached out your hand to rescue me.
A rainbow has appeared.
The Forget-me-nots have grown.

I will not forget your kind softly spoken voice.
Your love was a guiding light.
Comfort amongst the confusion.
I listened to your stories of your life.
And those who came before you, who told you theirs.
Days of pain of struggle.
Days of humour.
Days of youth.
Days of joy.
No more conversations on the telephone the silence is deafening, in my void of loss.
A rainbow has appeared.
The Forget-me-nots have grown.

Gifts of home-made jam, Sticky and sweet.
The smell of hot freshly baked mince pies on Christmas eve.

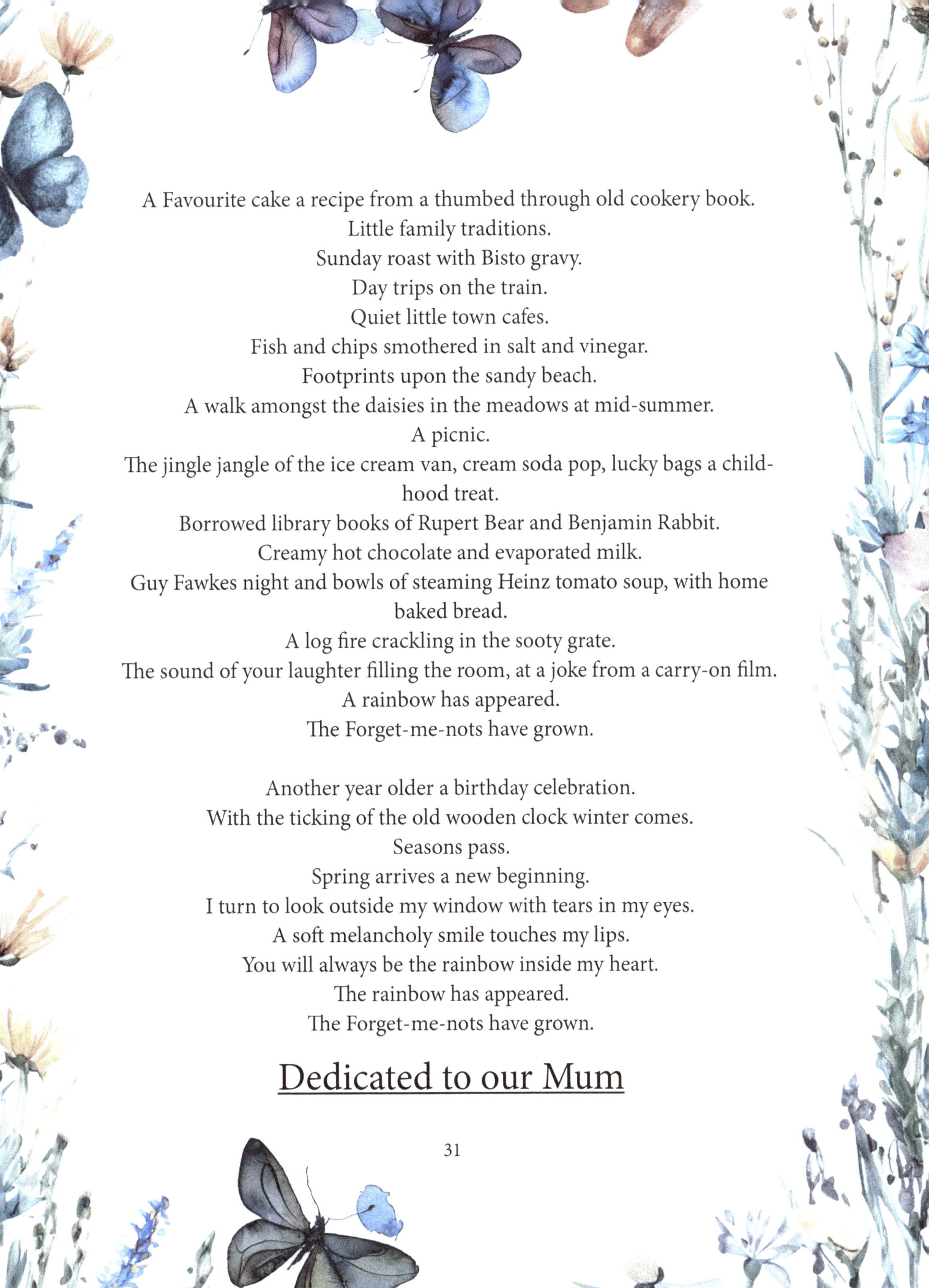

A Favourite cake a recipe from a thumbed through old cookery book.
Little family traditions.
Sunday roast with Bisto gravy.
Day trips on the train.
Quiet little town cafes.
Fish and chips smothered in salt and vinegar.
Footprints upon the sandy beach.
A walk amongst the daisies in the meadows at mid-summer.
A picnic.
The jingle jangle of the ice cream van, cream soda pop, lucky bags a childhood treat.
Borrowed library books of Rupert Bear and Benjamin Rabbit.
Creamy hot chocolate and evaporated milk.
Guy Fawkes night and bowls of steaming Heinz tomato soup, with home baked bread.
A log fire crackling in the sooty grate.
The sound of your laughter filling the room, at a joke from a carry-on film.
A rainbow has appeared.
The Forget-me-nots have grown.

Another year older a birthday celebration.
With the ticking of the old wooden clock winter comes.
Seasons pass.
Spring arrives a new beginning.
I turn to look outside my window with tears in my eyes.
A soft melancholy smile touches my lips.
You will always be the rainbow inside my heart.
The rainbow has appeared.
The Forget-me-nots have grown.

Dedicated to our Mum

The Pheonix

Phoenix rising,
Rising through the fire,
Rising
Higher
Higher.

Soaring through the flickering flame,
orange, red, yellow, purple, green.
Golden wings, lambent in the darkness of the night,
firebird in flight.
Bringing with her ray of light,
colours
changing
bright.

Phoenix has many names,
from continents their stories told.
To the believer,
young and old.

Phoenix, dreams growing,
elemental being.
Universal powers sowing,
her feet never touch upon the ground.
Firebird.
makes not a sound,
flames of desire,
higher
higher.

Dad's Poems

Written By Ron Allsopp for his little girl.

My Dad was a beautiful soul he taught me the magic of imagination and how it can take one to places beyond this earth , I call it the magic carpet ride of thought .but it is far more than that, it is vision, vision is everything, it's all an illusion what we see out there in the world is not as important as what we see from within, when we connect with the worlds within us we then can truly say we are connected to god's love and then a supernova of creativity collides with the soul.

A Daughter

In Springtime a daughter,
is like a budding rose,
In summer a warm meadow,
Of Wild flower,
In Autumn she is golden,
And rich as the changing leaves,
In winter she warms the heart,
And gives to the crystal snow a charm.

By the Fireside

Flickering Flickering,
Darting bright,
Red and yellow
Sparkling white,
Prancing shadows in my midst.
Ever changing shapes of smoke and mist,

My name ? I am a Flame,

The Fly

There is a fly upon the wall,
An enormous fly, its 6 feet tall,
The room is only five feet wide

He'd had a job to get inside,
He'd bent his head and flexed his knees,
And struggled in with little ease.

Now He's in and looked about,
He's realised he can't get out.

The Phanton Coach

On moonlit night each 23rd
Harness creaking can be heard.,
With sound of horn and coachman's cry,
The phantom coach for Staines goes by,
Clattering hooves and snorting steed,
Galloping on with all god speed,
See it not but hear it's sound,
The phantom coach is London bound.

The Cat

In the pot, out the pot,
Butterflies and that,
Isn't it a lovely life,
I'm glad that I'm a cat.

The Spell

Cats throughout the ages past,
Have with feline graces cast,
Their spell upon the human race,
And take there in their queenly place,

Snow

When the snow lays it's soft blanket on the fields at night.
There's quiet on the land,
A hush to touch the sensibilities of those,
With an inner feeling of infinity,
The moon masks the night,
With it's ghostly light.

Nothing moves, but, perhaps, a glimpse of a soft downed owl.
As it flits between the trees which with their leafless,
Branches raised in stark silhouette give rise,
To imaginings of witches and ogres,
When the snow lays it's soft blanket on the fields at night.

The Cathedral

Carols Flung towards the stars,
Welling from the heart,
Ancient spires proclaiming Christ,
Now let the battle start,
From this cathedral's majesty,
And from the souls within,
They will know who would deny,
That Christ shall conquer sin.

The Forest of Never

In the forest of never,
Across the Slendrous sea,
There lived a Whatsanella,
And a stripey bumble bee,
They lived on nectarina,
And furry wurry cake,
And they loved each other dearly,
As they sailed on the pink blue lake.

In the yellowed sky of never,
By clouds of pastel green,
There swooped the silver gander,
And birds of plasticine.
They heard the plans the lovers made,
In the quiet of a sunlit mist.
Saw the gentle tear of bumble bee.
When she and her lover kissed.

To the furthest bounds of never,
They carried the message gay,
That Whatsanella and bumble bee,
would marry on Jellimous day,
And all in the forest were joyful,
when they heard this wondrous news,
even the doleful Bumpies,
and the grumpy Figglydoos,

Plans were laid for the greatest feast.

The forest had ever seen,
All would be there on a wedding day,
To be graced by the faerie queen.

And the Rumpypuns came rolling,
The loopylegs flamfolling,
The Gigglewigs,
The Spikeytwigs,
The Tumbletags gambolling.

Then on the day the lovers wed,
With a feast and gifts galore,
The colourful crowds tumultuous voice,
Wished them love forever more,

And if one night in your dreams,
you cross the Slenderous sea,
you will meet there a Whatsanella,
and a stripey bumble bee.

Kittie's Plight

I Didn't know.
It was so high.
If I were a bird.
I could fly.
Down to the ground.
But now I'm bound.

To stay up here.
Until I pray.
Someone kindly comes my way.
And taking pity at the sight.
Of kitty in her tree bound plight.

This Beautiful book is a dedication to my dad, I wish to share with you a little about him. he loved the natural world the environment of nature's wonders, were important to him he had a vast knowledge about wildlife, trees, and flowers.

He used to take me on long country walks foraging for wild blackberries and crab apples which he would turn into delicious bramble jelly.
He was a logical man and was stimulated by topics where he could put his views across over a pint of Addlestones cider in the pub.

He was a member of Green Peace in the 1980's they were campaigning to protect whales. He gave to me a tape of Whale song which I found to be a fascinating listen and education of our precious Earth. Since then, we have become more aware of our planet and this is a good thing for our children's children, because now my brother takes his granddaughter on country walks too.

My dad loved outdoor activities such as cycling, running, badminton, walking and gardening. His favourite place was the craggy moors of Dartmoor and the views from the hills of the stars, he told me how luminous they were so clear in the night sky. He often went wild camping there enjoying the sounds around him of birds in the dawn chorus, his favourite bird was an Owl.

He was a Christian, he believed in a higher purpose of life, he often gave up his own time to help others in need. He became a full-time carer to nan Harriet the pain in his eyes was evident at the emotional strain he was under. It is tragic he too became inflicted with the same fate struck down by

Alzheimer's turning into Vascular Dementia in his seventies he passed away when he was 76 years old.

He visited those less fortunate, especially in the festive season, I remember an old lady who lived in a caravan across the meadows just off the beaten track of Lichfield city she was a gypsy, everyone knew her as old Bertha, Dad had known her through his walks. He took me to see her, she was delighted when she received a tin of biscuits from him, she invited us in for a cup of tea made from nettles being a child I found this quite an adventure.

Then there was old wizened Alf, who was well known around Lichfield because he was the mechanic who without any arms managed with his feet! When Alf became too frail and was skin and bones my dad, used to cook Christmas dinners for him.

My dad adored cats in fact he had three, a tortoiseshell and a Siamese but it was his long-haired Persian a ginger cat that became his mission to help, he found him as a stray, who used to come into the garden at the bungalow.

This cat's fur was matted, impossible to brush out, he took this cat in and nurtured him, he shaved off his fur so it would grow fluffy and healthy again, this cat he named Scruffy.

It broke my dad's heart when he had to put Scruffy down due to Kidney cancer, as Scruffy had bonded so well with him.

He never forgot that little cat, his poems he wrote were inspired by cats he had loved.

A special memory of my dad will always remain with me in the summer of 1976 he took me on a day out to Beacon Park in Lichfield city. Little did I know he had arranged a surprise for me a treasure hunt. He had tied little notes of white paper to the branches of bushes and tucked them inside and under rocks by the lake, the paper had clues on them for me to find the buried treasure and where it would lead me, he led me finally to an old tree opposite Beacon Street at last I had found it, my heart pounding with excitement.

I dug with a spoon dad had brought with him, oh my goodness it was a silver tea caddy I looked inside I saw an abundance of sparkling jewellery, brooches, necklaces and earrings, to a little girl it was like something from Aladdin's cave dad chuckled as he witnessed the joy upon my little face then his expression became serious, as he picked up an acorn that had fallen from the tree, his words to me were "That isn't the real treasure shall I tell you what it is"

"Yes Daddy"

"It is this little Acorn" then he hugged me.

He at that moment showed me what the most precious thing of all is our green land, and the cycle of nature within it which is connected to everything else.

We are nature we are not separate from it.

My dad died peacefully to the hymn of Silent Night he wouldn't get to see another Christmas I opened the letter he had left for me to be opened after his death.

The letter read.

Dear Ju don't be sad think of me as being in a joyful place were the evils of this world don't exist we will meet again in this place. I love you so much, and I am very proud of you, your compassionate nature your kindness.

Forget the difficulties of the past, look to the future you and Martin love and care for each other all will be well.

Remember some prayers have been answered find God through Jesus Christ, I cannot express how much I love you and always will my love, I wouldn't swap you for the world.

I wish you happiness and joy and peace all my love forever and ever.

Dad
God bless.

Dad's original Poetry work

In the forest of Never
Across the Blendrous Sea
There lived a Whatsanella
And a Stripey Bumble Bee.
They lived on Nectarina
And Furry Wurry cake
And they loved each other dearly
As they sailed on the Pink Blue Lake.

In the yellowed sky of Never
By clouds of pastel green
There swooped the Silver Gander
And Birds of Plastacing.
They heard the plans the lovers made
In the quiet of a sunlit mist
Saw the gentle tear of Bumble Bee
When she and her lover kissed.

To the furthest bounds of Never
They carried the message say
That Whatsanella and Bumble Bee
Would marry on Jellimous Day.
And all in the forest were joyful
When they heard this wonderous news
Even the doleful Bumpiei
And the grumpy Figglydoos.

Plans were laid for the greatest feast
The forest had ever seen
All would be there on a wedding day
To be graced by the Faerie Queen.

And the Rundypuns came rolling
The Loorylegs Flamfolling
The Gigglewigs
The Spikeytwigs
The Tumbletags gambolling.

Then on the day the lovers wed
With a feast and gifts galore
The colourful crowds tumultuous v
Wished them love forever more.

And if one night in your dreams
You cross the Blendrous Sea
You will meet there Whatsanella
And Stripey Bumble Bee.

To Ju
With Love

In springtime a daughter
Is like a budding rose;
In summer a warm meadow
Of wildflowers;
In autumn she is as golden
And rich as the changing leaves;
In winter she warms the heart
And gives to the crystal snow a charm.

IN THE POT, OUT THE POT
BUTTERFLIES AND THAT,
ISN'T IT A LOVELY LIFE,
I'M GLAD THAT I'M A CAT

I DIDN'T KNOW
IT WAS SO HIGH,
IF I WERE A BIRD
I COULD FLY
DOWN TO THE GROUND,
BUT NOW I'M BOUND
TO STAY UP HERE
UNTIL I PRAY
SOME ONE KINDLY
COMES MY WAY,
AND TAKING PITY
AT THE SIGHT
OF KITTY IN HER TREE –
BOUND PLIGHT,
GETS ME DOWN!

WHEN THE SNOW LAYS IT'S SOFT BLANKET ON THE FIELDS AT NIGHT,
THERE'S QUIET ON THE LAND.
A HUSH TO TOUCH THE SENSIBILITIES OF THOSE WITH
AN INNER FEELING OF INFINITY.
THE MOON MASKS THE NIGHT
WITH IT'S GHOSTLY LIGHT.
NOTHING MOVES, BUT, PERHAPS, A GLIMPSE OF A SOFT DOWNED OWL,
AS IT FLITS BETWEEN THE TREES WHICH, WITH THEIR LEAFLESS
BRANCHES RAISED IN STARK SILHOUETTE, GIVE RISE
TO IMAGININGS OF WITCHES AND OGRES.
WHEN THE SNOW LAYS IT'S SOFT BLANKET ON THE FIELDS AT NIGHT!

TO JU. WITH LOTS OF LOVE FROM DAD.

There is a fly upon the wall,
An enormous fly it's 6 feet tall,
The room is only five feet wide,
He'd had a job to get inside,
He'd bent his head and flexed his knees
And struggled in with little ease.
Now he's in and looked about,
He's realised he can't get out.

Cats throughout the ages past,
Have with feline graces cast,
Their spell upon the human race,
And take therein their queenly place.

The Phantom Coach

On moonlit night each 23rd,
Harness creaking can be heard;
With sound of horn and coachman's cry
The Phantom Coach for Staines goes by.
Clattering hooves and snorting steed
Galloping on with all god speed;
See it not but hear it's sound
The Phantom Coach is London bound.

Dedicated to the Memory of my Dad
Ronald Henry Allsop

ISBN 978-1-7385660-0-6

I would like to thank the people who helped me get this project off the ground, special thanks to my wonderful husband Martin Trevett who took the photos of the front and back cover, and I would like to thank him for the computer wizardry in helping to design the artwork of this book. I am sure I drove him crazy with my requests and ideas.

www.ingramcontent.com/pod-product-compliance
Lightning Source LLC
Chambersburg PA
CBHW042354070526
44585CB00028B/2932